THE JOURNEY CONTINUES

SAHILDEEP SINGH RAINA

Copyright © Sahildeep Singh Raina
All Rights Reserved.

TO
1.THE "ALMIGHTY GOD" my biggest inspiration
2.MY GRANDPARENTS who are giving me Blessings from above
3. My biggest strength : MY FAMILY

4. I also want to thank my sister "DR CHANDPREET KAUR" for being my constant motivator

Contents

Contents

Preface

This book is based on the poetry about life, its trials, the motivation and way out to succeed. And also about bonds of friendship, desires, PARENTAL LOVE and FAITH IN ALMIGHTY..

Acknowledgements

MY LOVE FOR POETRY WRITING continues with my SECOND BOOK.

A big thanks to my father "S. Parveen Singh Raina" & my mother "Mrs. Kulbir Kaur Raina" for inculcating positive beliefs in me.

I want to acknowledge the contribution of all my near and dear ones especially my parents, teachers, my sister, friends, my nephew and MY WIFE. All of you are my biggest support and constant motivators. Thank you ☺?☺?

My guide "DR. NEELIKA ARORA" for always being my biggest Source of Inspiration.. My teachers DR. SUVIDHA KHANNA & DR. PALLVI ARORA who have always been there for me when I needed them.

My Wife "MRS. RASMEET KAUR" for understanding me more than I understand myself.

My cute nephew "HRIDAAN SINGH" whose one smile encourages me all the time..

This acknowledgement is incomplete without the mention of two besties "DEVIA NANDA" & "ADITYA SALGOTRA" who are my constant support through THICK & THIN & always motivate me to WIN. MY colleagues of CLUSTER UNIVERSITY who are my BIGGEST CRITICS and MOTIVATORS and my sister DR. CHANDPREET KAUR who is always there for me..

ONE

OPPORTUNITIES: TRUTH AND DARE

There is a big arrival of so many seasons.
For all these seasons, there arise different reasons.
In the changing times, the opportunity also arises.
When there are opportunities, life brings huge surprises.
The surprises are always in the store.
The things in our destiny we cannot ignore.
When there is encouragement, it is when we get motivate.
The lost opportunity is when we create.
Life is a puzzle, sometimes reckless, sometime we handle with care.
In a particular moment, sometimes we choose truth, sometimes we choose dare.

TWO
TEACHERS

What is student's life without a teacher?
When there is no discipline, a student becomes wild creature.
Teacher's discipline brings a sense of relief.
When our confidence is down, there occurs a sense of belief.
A teacher is a mentor and she is a guide.
When she is with us, there cannot be any bumpy ride.
A teacher is big candle who always shines bright.
When darkness occurs big time, she gives her student light.
There is a sense of faith and hope.
When our morale is down our teacher holds it with tight rope.
A teacher fills all the empty voids that are there.
She is like another mother who gives us her full care.

THREE
OUR PARENTS

Our Parents are our biggest light.
When things become dark, their blessings shine bright.
Their blessings are our source of strength.
For our happiness they can go to any length.
All they want is our smile and care.
Our well-being is what they always want to hear.
It is for us only that their whole life is spent.
We can stand straight, that's why their backs get bent.
Life will always remain great when you have your mom & dad.
They will keep no stone unturned so that you never remain sad.

FOUR

THE APPROACH

Things get organized and in those times we get surprised.
The mirror is shown and we get know how much we grown.
The range is intact and we are gutsy to show contact.
The trouble therefore stops, all the sorrows get chops.
It is you who makes it direct and with efforts make it correct.
All you need is a small light.
And hope never gets out of your sight.
You have matured in a big way.
And when right time comes you will have your say.

FIVE

MY COUNTRY INDIA

India is a wonderful nation,
That has some wonderful creations.
It is called the wonder -land,
Where peace and harmony go hand in hand.
When there exists a symphony,
Here all the people live in harmony.
The country is land of sages.
But brave hearts exist in all ages.
How ancient is the Indian History,
There exists no mystery.
I feel proud of my nation,
Of its history, architecture and scientific creation.
The culture of which has grown so fast,
And whose heritage has reached very vast.

SIX

RACE AGAINST TIME

Life is a Race, which we have to face,
The troubles may be lot,
But we have to give everything we got.
The chances are to be handled with care,
So that we make everything bare.
Time and tide doesn't wait for any,
The chances are few, they are not many.
The race against time continues,
This race will never end.
To survive and succeed in life,
Our modesty should never end.

SEVEN
THE DESIRES

We all need a major flight.
And we will achieve when our intentions are right.
When the thoughts are good, there is nothing to worry
We will achieve what we want and we should not hurry.
The lines become clear and get easily located.
When the space required has been created.
We become aware with good sense.
The crowd of sorrow is removed and nothing remains
dense.
There is a requirement for things to remain in tandem.
Because some things that happen for us are very
random.
There is always a need to feel the fire.
And we must achieve what we desire.

EIGHT
THE TASKS

When your time will arrive, you will definitely sing your
song.
Sometimes you are right, sometimes you are wrong.
When you are right, there will always be love and
affection.
And you should be good in your thought and do your
task with perfection.
There should be no unnecessary thought and point to
linger.
When you do the task best, nobody will point finger.
The task will get tough; and you will have to be rough.
There will be no transparency, but you have to show
some decency.
The good days definitely arrive and we make efforts to
make them revive.
Make use of all the opportunities that are available.
If your time is there, you will definitely turn the table.

NINE

WOMAN'S DAY

The definition of woman has changed and will change
more.
It is ranging right to the core.
Nobody tends to understand the relativity.
It is up to her that how she shows her the creativity.
A woman shows many a face.
It is neither a competition nor a race.
She plays the role of mothers, daughters and wives.
In this alone time zone she plays many lives.
Woman is always considered to be epitome of greatness.
She never demands more and always expects less.
She never brings anything wrong to her sight.
And always tends to choose what is right.

TEN
BLESSINGS OF ALMIGHTY

There is a belief in God that keeps us motivated.
When the opportunities are lost, they get created.
All the troubles get solved.
And in totality we get fully evolved.
All the lost is thus found.
It is as amazing as a merry-go-round.
When you bow down in front of Almighty there is
nothing to worry.
Remain calm and composed and you should never be in
a hurry.
Sometimes life gives us different dance and song.
But when you have Blessings of Almighty, you can never
put any foot wrong.

ELEVEN

THE NEW TIMES AND TRENDS

We welcome the new time and trends.
We hope that there are meeting of our ends.
Let this time be good and also epic.
The things also change for good in a quick.
The trends change fast and are very furious.
They keep us informed and keep us curious.
Nothing lasts forever; there is always a shining light.
In these coming times let's hope that everything will
shine bright.
There are prayers that let each day be best.
And when we achieve our goals, only then we should
rest.

TWELVE

THE COMPLEXITIES

Life is a puzzle of questions that are very complex.
All these complex questions need a solution.
Very few questions get their meaning.
In this complex world, they are leaning.
All of this needs a proper start.
Even for this, we need to have a big heart.
The heart of gold which is easy to hold.
The huge difference is therefore seen.
The complexities end when your intentions are clean.

THIRTEEN

MOTHER'S DAY

The definition of mother is not in any book.
She provides her child a new outlook.
The things are when tough, she is that big rope.
When we feel hopeless, she is like a ray of hope.
Nobody can fill her empty void.
Her blessings are such which nobody can avoid.
She is a gift, which makes us uplift.
And with her sense, she sees how much we are tense.
Mother's Day is just a day to show how much do we care.
Because mother is that gift of God which is very rare.

FOURTEEN
THE REALITY

The world and us, sometimes dissimilar and sometimes
same.
The patterns are different, just like a cat-mouse game.
We want to survive; perfection is always we always
thrive.
Hoping for the better things, the bad omen hopefully
never stings.
The reality is crude, sometimes happy, and sometimes
rude.
But we always thrive for excellence, especially in the
proper sense.
The job is to win and strive big.
And ignore those who are taking your dig.
The reality of life is to get better and strong
That's where you will always last really long.

FIFTEEN

FAITH: A BEAUTIFUL THING

Always be God-Fearing, when you are in trouble he is
always hearing.
The troubles may cause us to break, but life is never a
piece of cake.
The change is true and important to the core.
The less we think, what we get is more.
Be bold, brave and always daring.
And we should never stop caring.
The time is changing and taking a rapid stride.
It is up to us that it never becomes a bumpy ride.
Take the blessings of Lord and have belief.
This belief will always bring a sense of relief.

SIXTEEN

THE RACE AGAINST TIME

The race against time is so tough.
It may therefore make us little rough.
The time always shows the change.
If we have to survive, we have to show our change.
There are no charges, there is no rent.
But to survive well we have to motivate ourselves
hell-bent.
The changes in nature are similar to changes in whom
and what we are.
And we have to transform our scars to stars.
Even sky has its limits, it is also in sanction.
When we know our limits, we get the right direction.
Life need not be a puzzle and we all want chances.
The times changes very fast and there are no easy
dances.

SEVENTEEN

THE ALMIGHTY LORD

When there is almighty Lord, there exists hope.
When there is hope, there exists desire.
The desire keeps us motivated, it keeps us better.
'Prayer' is such a small motivating letter.
Lord is the supreme Power.
Among the high tides, he helps to stand like a tower.
With hope there is a desire to succeed.
No matter even if someone degrades you, continue your
good deed.
Life is there to make, break and create.
Oh Almighty! You are the ultimate.

EIGHTEEN
A TRUE FRIEND

What is a friend, how is he defined?
When two mates meet, a friendship is refined.
A friend is sweet, he is smart,
He touches your chords, he melts your heart.
A true friend is always cherished,
When he is with me, all my sorrows are perished.
A true friend brings trust and he brings care,
Nothing can change the bond we share.
A true friend takes you to the cloud nine,
He is indeed your lifeline.
A true friend is the one, who cares for your smile,
And for that purpose, he can even go to mile.

NINETEEN
LIFE AND ITS CHALLENGES

Life is a race, which we have to face.
Times do change; this is when we show our range.
When everything lies beneath, we cannot go
underneath.
Face your fears like many wars.
And transform your scars to stars.
Life is a challenge which never ends.
And by showing our strength, we should never bend.
Be a winner and stand like a tower.
Never give up and show the real will-power.
Life and its challenges shall continue forever.
But if we give up our self-confidence will raise never.

TWENTY
LIFE AND ITS THOUGHTS

The troubles may be true, but we cannot quit.
In these situations, we have to show our charm and wit.
We have to motivate ourselves and keep moving ahead.
We have to work hard and also remain stead.
Arrogance is a big deceiver, appreciation is a big
receiver.
We have to keep our feet firmly to the ground.
Or the things may turn awry, like a huge big round.
Life is a lesson, which we learn.
Because of the ongoing experiences which we earn.
Keep all the positivity, have all the negative things way.
Just a one good thought would make your day.

TWENTY-ONE
UNDERSTANDING ONESELF

You understand what is good and bad.
But then also we cannot be sad.
This understanding makes her very curious.
And we don't have to remain furious.
Only times want to change fast.
As long as our range last.
Excellence is the key in whatever we do or make.
It is always like give and take.
We should understand the skill and increase our will.
The understanding always gives us total benefits.

TWENTY-TWO

DESIRE: THE NEVER –ENDING STORY

There are many stories, which are to be told.
When we understand good and bad, everything is put in hold.
These stories are special, these stories are better.
Sometimes they form a paragraph, sometimes they form a letter.
There is an exchange of wonderful thought.
We understand the values which we have bought.
The time flies so quickly in just a fraction.
We have no time left to give our reaction.
What matters then most is our approach towards the change.
This is the time that we show our real range.
When we are mentally strong, then nothing is going to be wrong.

Because when we have that inner desire, we can even fight fire-for- fire.

TWENTY-THREE
BATTLE

The battle always exist, sometimes fair, sometimes unfair.
The trouble may be high, we cannot return back to
square.
Silence is gold; this is what we should always hold.
There is always a desire; we cannot burn our hands in
fire.
You want to fly, you want to get ahead.
But it's not as easy as putting butter on the bread.
Survival is the key and it should click.
When your battle starts, you shouldn't flick.
It's true that this is a battle of survival and death.
That will be continued till our last breath.

TWENTY-FOUR
THE SURVIVAL INSTINCT

There is an existence that really tends to exist.
When our approach becomes pragmatic, all thoughts
come in our list.
The list is sometimes huge and it is sometimes small.
Things become so complicated that we talk to the
fourth wall.
The troubles create a huge void.
Actually, these are like meteors and asteroid.
Comparisons are quickly broken and made.
It is the exchange of emotional trade.
The thought changes all and can turn us better.
And can transform our ordinary day into a red-letter.

TWENTY-FIVE
THE LAST SONG

This is the last song, which I will sing.
I wonder why I am standing in the middle of the ring.
The questions are plenty, answers are few.
And now all my returns are due.
This summer hopefully things will change.
We will be able to showcase our range.
The song would depict all my emotions.
And it will also break all stereotypes and notions.
I cannot be critical all the while.
Even when situation is tough, all I need is to put a smile.

www.ingramcontent.com/pod-product-compliance
Lightning Source LLC
Chambersburg PA
CBHW021329160726
47994CB00004B/1684